THE NEED TO KNOW LIBRARY™

EVERYTHING YOU NEED TO KNOW ABOUT

CONFRONTING

VIOLENCE AGAINST WOMEN

ALEXIS BURLING

Rosen
YA™
New York

Published in 2019 by The Rosen Publishing Group, Inc.
29 East 21st Street, New York, NY 10010

Library of Congress Cataloging-in-Publication Data

Names: Burling, Alexis, author.
Title: Everything you need to know about confronting violence
against women / Alexis Burling.
Description: New York : Rosen Publishing, 2019 | Series: The
need to know library | Includes bibliographical references and
index. | Audience: Grades 7–12.
Identifiers: LCCN 2017045731| ISBN 9781508179160 (library
bound) | ISBN 9781508179252 (pbk.) Subjects: LCSH: Women—
Violence against—Juvenile literature. | Abused women—Juvenile
literature.
Classification: LCC HV6250.4.W65 B868 2019 | DDC
362.88082—dc23
LC record available at https://lccn.loc.gov/2017045731

CONTENTS

INTRODUCTION

For many teens, prom is one of the most exhilarating times in high school. There's the shopping for the perfect outfit, the fancy dinner before the party, the dancing the night away. But for eighteen-year-old Micah Jeppesen, the experience was different. In 2015, just before the evening of her senior prom began, her boyfriend of more than a year slapped her in the face during an argument. Then he threw her to the ground.

Jeppesen was shaken. Though her boyfriend was often critical and possessive of her at times, she assumed the violent act was an isolated occurrence. It wasn't. A few weeks later, the couple got into a fight while driving home from a graduation party. The yelling escalated and Jeppesen's boyfriend snapped. He shoved her head into the car window and started to choke her. Jeppesen bolted out of the car, but her boyfriend caught up with her. He grabbed her by the hair and dragged her on the ground while punching her in the face.

Luckily, Jeppesen escaped. When she got home, her father called the police. Her boyfriend was arrested and sentenced to thirty days in jail. Upon his release, he was ordered to attend anger-management sessions. But Jeppesen couldn't forget what happened. "I thought I was going to lose my life," she told her local Minnesota paper, the *River Falls Journal*. "I was scared that he had a nut loose. ... I didn't expect him to do something like that."

At a rally in Spain in 2015, hundreds of thousands of women protested gender-based violence. Today, vitally important demonstrations like this one are held all over the world.

After the incident, Jeppesen broke up with her boyfriend. But that was only a small part of the moving-on process. She was diagnosed with post-traumatic stress disorder (PTSD) and sought counseling in order to cope with destructive thoughts. Loud voices became a trigger point. Learning to date again proved difficult.

But in time, Jeppesen began to heal. She volunteered at the HOPE Coalition—an organization that helps victims of domestic and sexual violence, child abuse, and homelessness get back on their feet—and started speaking to high school students about how to spot and confront violent relationships. She also enrolled in college to pursue a nursing degree.

Jeppesen was the victim of a horrific crime, but she extricated herself from the situation and slowly learned how to form healthier relationships. But some women and girls aren't that fortunate. According to the World Health Organization (WHO), about one out of every three women worldwide—about 35 percent—have experienced either physical and/or sexual intimate-partner violence or non-partner sexual violence in their lifetimes. Many of these women endure the punishment for years before they can escape. Others don't survive the trauma.

The United Nations (UN) defines violence against women as "any act of gender-based violence that results in, or is likely to result in, physical, sexual, or mental harm or suffering to women, including threats of such acts, coercion or arbitrary deprivation of liberty, whether occurring in public or in private life." It is a violation of basic human rights and affects women of all ages and gender identities, all ethnicities and races, and female members of any economic class with any level of education. Violence against women and girls is global—and widespread.

But when armed with accurate information and sufficient tools, there are ways to combat the problem. By understanding what violence against women is, why it happens, and how to get help if you or someone you know or love is involved in a psychologically, physically, or sexually violent situation, you can be better prepared to prevent an attack from occurring—or cope with it when it does. With action and perseverance, it is possible to make this world a better, safer place for women and girls.

CHAPTER ONE

WHAT IS VIOLENCE AGAINST WOMEN?

In 2015, a news story about R&B singer Rihanna sent ripples through the pop culture universe. That November, she was interviewed for the cover of *Vanity Fair*. In the article, she revealed her long-repressed feelings about the incident that earned her the reputation of being a "poster girl" for domestic violence.

Six years earlier, Rihanna was attacked by her then-boyfriend, R&B singer Chris Brown. The night before the Grammy Awards, he assaulted her in his car. Gruesome pictures of Rihanna's bruised face and arms were leaked to the media. She was hospitalized. Brown was arrested, charged with battery, issued a restraining order, and sentenced to six years' probation. Rihanna and Brown broke up—but three years later, in 2012, they got back together.

"I was that girl—that girl who felt that as much pain as this relationship is, maybe some people are built stronger than others," Rihanna told *Vanity Fair*. "Maybe I'm the person who's almost the guardian angel to this person, to be there when they're not strong enough … when they just

Rihanna has inspired millions of girls to be proud and feel confident about themselves. But even she has struggled with abuse.

need someone to encourage them in a positive way and say the right thing."

Rihanna's fans were confused. She was beautiful, ultratalented, and one of the most famous musicians in the world. Why did she take back the man who abused her?

The couple's second time around didn't last long. Rihanna realized the unhealthiness of the situation. Later that year, she and Brown broke up for the final time. "If you put up with [bad behavior], maybe you are agreeing that you [deserve] this, and that's when I finally had to say, 'Uh-oh, I was stupid thinking I was built for this,'" Rihanna said. "Sometimes you just have to walk away."

TYPES OF VIOLENCE AGAINST WOMEN

Rihanna's suffering at the hands of an abusive partner is just one example of the type and degree of violence inflicted on women and girls every day all over the world. Violence against women can be physical, sexual, psychological, emotional, or verbal. It can be perpetrated by an intimate partner—someone male or female who has a romantic relationship with the victim—or by a total stranger. It can happen at school, home, work, or on the street and can take on a variety of forms including, but not limited to, domestic violence, child abuse, dating violence, stalking, or online abuse via social media, aggressive emails, or texts.

Violence in relationships occurs when one person wields power and control over a partner and chooses to act aggressively in order to keep that control. The following are some of the most common types of violence women and girls might encounter.

PHYSICAL VIOLENCE

According to the United Nations, the most common type of violence women and girls face is physical violence inflicted by an intimate partner. This means that women are more likely to experience physical abuse by someone they know closely—a current or former spouse, boyfriend or girlfriend, dating partner or sexual partner in a heterosexual or same-sex relationship—than by a stranger who might attack them in a park or rob them for money. In fact, a study done by the National Coalition Against Domestic Violence reports that one out of every four women in the United States is severely physically abused by an intimate partner during her lifetime.

Nearly one-third of women worldwide who have been in a relationship have also experienced some form of physical and/or sexual violence by their intimate partner in their lifetime.

Physical violence can also take place in nonsexual domestic relationships. Some examples might be a father that beats up his daughter every time her homework isn't done on time, a drunken uncle who hits his niece when her parents are away, or an older brother who pummels his sister with his fists when she doesn't do what he says. Though it's less common, female relatives can be aggressors too. Kicking, biting, slapping, punching, whipping, hair pulling, smashing dishes, and breaking furniture are just some of the methods used by abusers.

MALTREATMENT AROUND THE WORLD

In the United States and Canada, the majority of women and girls who are physically violated experience child, domestic, or sexual abuse. But in parts of Asia, Africa, and some parts of South America, other types of abuse are also prevalent. The following are examples of the types of violence women face around the world.

- Female genital cutting is a ritualized practice in which part or all of the external female genitalia is removed for nonmedical reasons. According to the World Health Organization, more than two hundred million girls and women alive today in thirty countries across Africa, the Middle East, and Asia are victims. The practice can have severe health consequences, including excessive bleeding and death.
- Early marriage occurs when a girl under the age of eighteen is forced to marry an older man against her will. More than likely, she will also become pregnant or catch a sexually transmitted disease, including HIV. According to UNICEF, more than 700 million women who are alive today got married before they turned eighteen. About 250 million of those were younger than fifteen.
- Honor killing refers to the murder of a girl or woman because of her perceived disgrace to her family's or community's "honor." It can happen if she is accused of premarital sex, cheating on her husband, acting outside the prescribed religious or cultural behavioral norms (such as leaving the house without a male relative), or if she is raped.

SEXUAL ABUSE AND RAPE

In some cases, physical violence can turn sexual. Perpetrators can be strangers, but they might also be intimate partners, members of the family, or trusted members of the community. Targets of sexual assault are kissed, groped, fondled, or otherwise molested by a partner without their consent. Those who are forced to perform sexual intercourse against their will are raped. In particularly egregious cases, rape victims are tied up, strangled, or knocked unconscious during sexual acts. According to the U.S. Department of Health's Office on Women's Health, more than twenty-three million women in the Unit-

It is common for couples to fight. Even the best-matched couples argue sometimes. But threats and violence are never OK. There is always another solution.

ed States have been raped. Most of these women were younger than twenty-five when the rape took place. Nearly half of them were under eighteen.

Contrary to popular belief, sexual violence doesn't have to be physical. Some sexual abusers restrict their partners' access to birth control or poke holes in condoms in order to exert control. Others ply their girlfriends with alcohol or date rape drugs like Rohypnol or ketamine to lower their defenses and impair their ability to make responsible decisions. Even if these behaviors occur within a dating relationship, they are still considered sexual abuse or rape if consent is not given by both partners.

SEX TRAFFICKING: A GLOBAL EPIDEMIC

Sex trafficking is a form of modern slavery that exists across the globe. It occurs when a person uses physical violence, verbal threats, or financial bondage to force women and girls to become prostitutes, mail-order brides, exotic dancers, or participants in pornography against their will. Sex trafficking targets can be any age, race, gender identity, or sexual orientation.

In the United States, any minor under age eighteen forced to perform sexual acts for a commercial purpose is a victim of sex trafficking. The most vulnerable girls and women are homeless runaways and sufferers of domestic violence or sexual assault. According to the International Labor Organization, at least 20.9 million adults and children are sold worldwide into commercial sexual slavery and forced labor. Women and girls make up 98 percent of victims of trafficking for sexual exploitation.

PSYCHOLOGICAL AND EMOTIONAL VIOLENCE

When you hear the term "violence," it's often assumed that a physical act of aggression has taken place. But in many cases, women and girls are bullied without being touched. Some are stalked by obsessive partners or by someone they don't know. Examples of stalking include when someone repeatedly contacts you when you don't want him or her to, follows you, knows your schedule, sends you gifts, or threatens you or your loved ones.

Every year, 6.6 million people are stalked in the United States. Women are nearly three times more likely to be stalked than men. A majority are stalked before they turn twenty-five.

Teen girls are especially vulnerable to emotional and psychological bullying. Some are targeted because of their race or sexual orientation. Others are made fun of because of their clothes, their grades, or the way they look and act. The abuse often starts out verbal and turns physical. More often than not, victims are also bullied online via Facebook, Instagram, Snapchat, and other social media sites. These social-harassment campaigns can become so brutal that they trigger devastating consequences, such as a victim's suicide.

THE BOTTOM LINE

Whether it's physical or psychological, violence of any kind is a serious, life-altering occurrence. Unfortunately, it is not uncommon for women and girls who endure one form of violence to also experience other types— not just once, but repeatedly over a period of time. Usually their abusers exhibit a range of troubling behavior, including jealousy and possessiveness, manipulation, coercion, rage, or an inability to control their emotions. These actions are designed to control, blame, humiliate, or induce fear and may result in permanent injuries to their victims or death.

So why do so many women fall prey to such sadistic behavior? One thing is certain: violence against women is never excusable and never the victim's fault. There are many contributing factors that can help explain why violence against women is so prevalent, not just in the United States and Canada, but around the world.

CHAPTER TWO

WHY DOES VIOLENCE AGAINST WOMEN HAPPEN?

I n 2000, Liz Luras was about to make the change of a lifetime. She had just graduated from high school and had enlisted in the U.S. Army. After scoring above average on the aptitude tests, she was assigned to do intelligence work and given top-secret clearance. During her training at boot camp, she impressed the staff sergeants so much that she was recommended for West Point, the top military academy in the United States.

"It was the most exciting time," Luras told the non-profit group Human Rights Watch. "I felt so empowered as a patriot, soldier and woman."

But for Luras, a long, celebrated career in the military was not to be. On the night of the Marine Corps ball, she was raped by her date. Without checking with Luras, a colleague reported the incident to Luras's superiors. Luras told her father, who contacted a congressman about the assault.

The backlash was swift and immediate. Though Luras was taken to a hospital and questioned by military and civilian police, her rapist was never charged

MARINES UNITED: A FACEBOOK SCANDAL

According to a report issued by the U.S. Department of Defense, US military service members came forward about 6,172 cases of sexual assault in 2016. In that same report, an anonymous survey revealed that 14,900 service members experienced some form of sexual assault in 2016, from unwanted touching to rape. But as with many types of violence perpetrated against women, not all abuse in military circles is physical.

On March 4, 2017, reporter and Marine veteran Thomas Brennan broke the shocking story about a men-only Facebook group called Marines United. Consisting of nearly 30 thousand members, the group posted and shared more than 130 thousand photos of naked female service members and veterans without their consent. In many cases, these women were identified by their full name and rank, as well as their social media handles.

Four months later, the first U.S. Marine was tried for his participation in the scandal. He pleaded guilty and was sentenced to ten days confinement. His rank was reduced, and he was forced to give up two-thirds of his monthly salary.

with any crime. When Luras returned to duty, she was sexually harassed by male recruits and slut-shamed by female friends of the rapist. Her supervisors forced her to clean toilets and do push-ups until she vomited. Worst of all, Luras was raped twice more. She didn't breathe a word about any of it. "The retaliation was so terrible," Luras said. "I was more afraid of the retaliation than of being raped."

Eventually, Luras was discharged from the army— for having a so-called personality disorder. Her money for college and benefits were revoked. Because of the "PD" designation, she was turned down for jobs and, at times, suffered through bouts of homelessness because of lack of work. It took more than ten years for Luras to regain her self-confidence. In 2013, she spoke out about what happened at the Truth and Justice Summit in Washington, D.C. "I was raped for my country. I was discredited for my country. I fought for freedom. I'm still fighting for freedom," she said.

FACTORS CONTRIBUTING TO VIOLENCE AGAINST WOMEN

Women have been serving in the U.S. military in some capacity for more than a century. More women were on the military payroll in August 2016 than ever before— approximately 15.5 percent. But the sad reality is that many female service members continue to be victims of psychologically, physically, and sexually violent crimes.

The problem isn't limited to the military. Sexual misconduct is pervasive, as seen in the 2017 takedown of prominent figures such as Harvey Weinstein, Matt Lauer, Charlie Rose, Mark Halperin, and Roy Moore, sexual harassment, unwanted groping, and rape have been going on for decades in the entertainment industry, the media, and in many areas of U.S. government.

About 8,600 women in the US military were sexually assaulted in 2016. One in four of these women were targeted by someone in their chain of command.

Women and girls in all walks of life are vulnerable to violence. The following are just a few of the factors that contribute to violence against women and explain why it's such a widespread phenomenon.

GENDER ROLES AND SEXISM

Violence against women is rooted in unequal power relationships between men and women. In many cultures, women are responsible for taking care of the home and

In 2017, a group of New Yorkers gathered to protest discrimination against LGBTQ people. All members of the LGBTQ community deserve equal respect and equal rights.

raising children while men go to work, earn money, and make all the decisions. This creates an inequity within the family structure and an incorrect perception that women are weaker or should be subservient. In some places like parts of Pakistan and India, it's excusable for husbands to beat or murder their wives if it's perceived that they're being disrespectful. In areas of South Asia where dowry requirements are substantial, baby girls are killed to prevent a financial burden to the family.

Outside the home, women face other challenges. Cissexism—discrimination against transgender people—and violence against lesbians are common in cultures where heterosexuality is the norm. Sexism and misogyny—an ingrained prejudice against women and the belief that men are superior—are, too. Because women are sometimes objectified by the media— airbrushed photos in magazines, ads featuring scantily clad women to sell products, derogatory song lyrics— the notion of woman as sex object has also become more acceptable. Young girls looking for models on how to behave or dress often associate "overtly sexy" with "cool," leaving them open to unwanted attention from predators.

EDUCATION, ECONOMIC INEQUALITY, AND LACK OF OPPORTUNITY

In many countries, girls don't have the same access to education as boys. Without the necessary skills, girls have less freedom, less choice, and less chance of getting ahead or succeeding in a career. Sometimes this leaves them more vulnerable to violence. In extreme cases, just the act of pursuing an education can be life threatening for girls, as in the near-lethal 2012 attack on Pakistani education activist Malala Yousafzai.

In places where women aren't barred from going to school and getting an advanced degree, most women still earn less than men over the course of their careers. According to a 2015 Pew Research Center study, women in the United States make 83 percent less than men in median hourly earnings. In many industries, women

Malala Yousafzai has continued to speak out about the importance of education for girls since winning the Nobel Peace Prize in 2014.

are routinely passed over for leadership roles or promotions. A lack of opportunity and sufficient income can sometimes lead to homelessness or the need to take desperate measures, such as prostitution, to stay afloat.

RACISM AND OTHER PREJUDICES

Sexism is sometimes exacerbated by other prejudices, such as racism, homophobia, and ableism. Immigrant women or girls of color are often looked down upon, discriminated against, or don't receive the same opportunities as their white counterparts. Lack of resources increases their risk of abuse, exploitation, or violent relationships due to economic dependency or limited income-earning options. For example, a report released by the United Nations showed that indigenous women in Canada are five times more likely than other women of the same age to die as the result of violence.

Disabled women are also frequently targeted for violence. According to the Office on Women's Health in the U.S. Department of Health and Human Services, women with disabilities are more likely to be victims of sexual assault or domestic violence than women without disabilities. Some caregivers withhold medicine or refuse to bathe and feed mentally or physically incapacitated patients. The United Nations reports that in North America, Europe, and Australia, more than half of women with disabilities have experienced physical abuse, compared to one-third of non-disabled women.

Women and girls of color often deal with a toxic blend of racism and sexism that is even worse than the sexism their white peers face.

THE FLIP SIDE

Research shows that poverty, a lack of access to education, and racial and gender-identity biases are just some of the major reasons why women and girls become victims of violence. The same factors also influence those who inflict violence on others. Abusers are more likely to be less educated and less economically stable. In some instances, they are also less accepting of immigrants, people of color, and members of the LGBTQ community. Many boys and men who perpetrate violence also grew up in violent households and carry the learned behavior forward. Some frequently abuse alcohol or drugs.

Understanding why violence against women and girls occurs makes it easier to prevent in the future. But it is important to remember that risk factors are not definite links. For example, a boy who watches his father abuse his mother will not necessarily follow the same path later in life. For the same reason, just because a woman has an Ivy League education and a high-paying job doesn't mean she's immune to domestic violence. Violence against women is a complex, layered social and economic issue that extends across societies, cultures, and borders.

MYTHS AND FACTS

MYTH: Abuse happens only in "problem" families, to ethnic minorities, to uneducated or less educated people, and in poorer areas.

ACT: Violence against women and girls can happen regardless of race, class, income, ethnicity, sexual orientation, gender identity, or level of intelligence. It can happen anywhere, at any time.

MYTH: People who abuse women and girls are easily identifiable.

ACT: Abusers come in all shapes and sizes. They can be rich or poor, sober or a substance abuser, from a healthy or troubled family. Some abuse intimate partners, family members, or friends. Others abuse strangers.

MYTH: In some situations, women and girls who are psychologically, verbally, or sexually abused ask for it, provoke it, want it, or deserve it.

FACT: No matter how a woman is acting, what she says, or what she is wearing in any situation, violence perpetrated against her is never acceptable under any circumstances.

CHAPTER THREE

GETTING HELP

L et's do an experiment. Think of your best friend. Maybe you have been friends since elementary school. You like the same music, shop at the same stores, read the same types of books. You know each other's favorite food—and each other's deepest secrets.

But lately it has seemed like something's off. Since her mother and stepfather got back together a few months ago, your best friend has been uncharacteristically quiet every time you get together. She doesn't crack her usual corny jokes, doesn't smile, and rarely answers the phone when you call. The last time you hung out, she had bruises on her arm. What gives?

While none of these signs point unequivocally to an abusive situation, chances are high that something is not right with your pal. Maybe she's going through a difficult semester and needs more time to study. It's also possible that something serious is going on at home—and it likely has to do with her newly resurfaced stepfather.

So what do you do? Do you approach her about it? Talk to someone at school? Call the police?

Depending on the situation and its severity, there are many paths you can take if you or someone you know

If something seems off with your friend, the worst thing you can do is ignore it. Try asking questions. But tread lightly. She may not feel comfortable sharing her feelings.

is or has been involved in a violent situation. Each has benefits and drawbacks, and each comes with its own set of risks. Whatever you choose, remember to stay safe and be mindful of your limitations. Talking to someone and getting help is often the hardest step, but the rewards are well worth it.

STAY SAFE

Violence can happen anytime, anywhere. While it's impossible to prevent all violent behavior from crossing

KNOW THE SIGNS

When you are in a volatile relationship with a partner, parent or guardian, or friend—or suspect someone you know is—it can be tricky to know what to do. First, try to identify whether the situation is just a regular argument or if it is, or will likely become, violent and dangerous. Here are signs to watch out for that signify abuse.

- **Controlling behavior:** Abusers want power over their victims. They use blame, shame, threats, and insults to get what they want. They can be jealous, moody, possessive, and irrational. Some isolate their victims from loved ones to maintain control.
- **Unreasonable expectations:** Abusers often expect their victims to be perfect. Many demand perfect grades, perfect looks, perfect behavior, or perfect home-cooked meals. Most will not take no for an answer.
- **Promises to change:** Abusers never think violent behavior is their fault. They also frequently promise to change. The phrase "I promise I'll never do it again" is a sure sign of a violent relationship.
- **Bruises:** Abusers leave scars. They lash out in whatever way is most effective—by physically hurting their victims or stifling their personalities. If bruises are visible—whether emotional, psychological, or physical—the situation has already become violent.
- **Too many excuses:** Abusers are master manipulators. They do what they want, when they want, how they want. Sometimes their victims don't know how to break the abusive cycle. They make excuses for why the abuser's behavior is somehow OK. But it's not.

your path or the paths of your loved ones, there are some precautions you can take. If you are out late at night, never walk home alone after dark. Travel with a buddy or call a taxi or car service to take you where you need to go. Carry a whistle on your key chain and keep pepper spray in your bag. No preparation is too small.

Staying mindful on the internet is also key. Sure, it might be fun for you and your pals to post pics of yourselves in sexy outfits on Facebook or Instagram. But think about who might see those photographs and what impression they might get. Never post something you wouldn't want your mom or a job recruiter to see. Keep

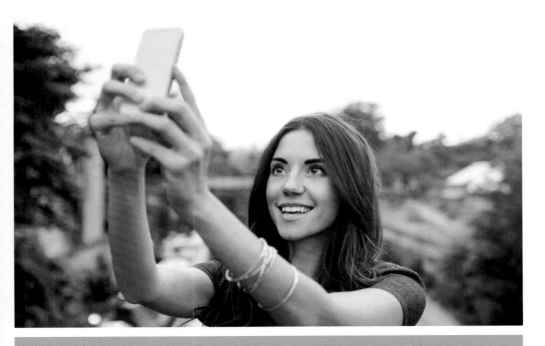

Social media is all about good times. But be mindful of what you post. Steer clear of potentially harmful confrontations and posting damaging or incriminating content.

privacy settings on all apps up to date. Never give personal information out to strangers. If someone is stalking you or saying nasty things about you, defriend or block that person immediately. Contact the site's administrator. Whatever you do, never engage. Communicating with a stalker or abuser will only reinforce the behavior.

No matter what situation you're in—whether it's at a party where there's alcohol, on a date gone wrong, or at home with a hot-blooded parent or guardian—having the phone numbers of people you trust programmed into your phone or on speed dial is essential for reaching help when you need it quickly. In violent situations, a few saved seconds can make a big difference if you need to reach out for help.

WHEN TO GET INVOLVED

If you stumble upon an abusive situation happening to a friend or stranger, it can be terrifying. Your first impulse might be to step in and try to stop whatever's happening. But sometimes getting involved might make the situation worse for the victim. You could also put yourself in danger.

The safest way to de-escalate a violent situation is to call for professional help. After you've done so—and as long as the perpetrator doesn't have a weapon—here are two tips you might follow:

- If you see a woman or girl being targeted, remain at the scene at a safe distance. The abuser might be less likely to continue or escalate the violence if he or she knows there are witnesses.

- Take power away from the abuser by speaking directly to the victim. Ask questions such as "Are you OK?" or "Is there anything I can do to help?" This not only reassures the victim that she is not alone and you are there to help, it also gives you clues about how serious the situation is.

ALERT AUTHORITIES

The most important thing to remember about violence perpetrated against women and girls is that victims should never be blamed for what happened. Whether it's a one-time or ongoing event, a domestic or child abuse case, dating violence, or online harassment, it's always the abuser's fault. Still, it can be daunting to try to stop the violence from occurring.

A wise step to take, even if it's scary, is to tell someone. If you're the one being abused, share what happened with a trusted friend. If the violence is happening at school, at work, online, or with a boyfriend or girlfriend and you feel comfortable talking to your parents or a guardian, do so. A school administrator or guidance counselor is another viable option. Confiding in one or more of these people lets them know you not only trust their advice, but you also trust them as a person. Be clear about whether you want suggestions about what to do or just want their emotional support.

Police officers are trained to treat domestic or sexual violence calls as potentially life-threatening situations. Your safety is their top priority.

If you're not ready to talk to someone you know about what's happening, there are local rape crisis centers, domestic violence shelters, and national hotlines that staff trained counselors who help victims develop a safety plan or get away from an abuser. The National Domestic Violence Hotline (1-800-799-SAFE) is one. The National Sexual Assault Hotline (1-800-656-HOPE) is another. The Love Is Respect Hotline is intended specifically for teens (1-866-331-9474). All calls are free.

Sometimes violent situations against women and girls are life threatening. If this is the case, more drastic measures are in order. If you've been physically hurt, go to the hospital to make sure your health isn't in jeopardy. If you witness an attack on the street, call the police immediately. If you or someone you know is being abused by a parent or guardian, a phone call to Child Protective Services is your best bet. They are responsible for receiving and investigating reports of suspected child abuse and neglect. Get ready to provide evidence of any abuse you've experienced or witnessed.

No matter which path you choose, taking action to prevent violence can be frightening. In addition to a family member or other trusted authority, there are still others who can help you make informed decisions. Legal service providers are trained professionals who can help you create the best and safest plan for what to do next, such as filing a restraining order. Victims' advocates help those in abusive situations find the resources they need to move forward, including information on how to press legal charges. They work in community organizations, police stations, and legal offices.

If you or someone you know encounters violence against women or girls, alerting the proper authorities can help solve the problem. But it's only half the battle. The other crucial element is learning how to cope—and hopefully heal.

CHAPTER FOUR

LEARNING TO COPE

Witnessing or enduring violence in any form—whether mental, emotional, or physical—is torture on the mind and body. But once help is secured, there's another component that's essential to recovery: figuring out how to cope. Finding adequate time and space to heal is crucial—no matter how long it might take.

If you or someone you know has experienced violence, it's important to know that just because the event is over, the body and brain might still be experiencing trauma. Not every person will share the same symptoms. But each reaction, while maybe not ideal and sometimes painful, is normal given the circumstances. Many abuse victims and bystanders suffer from insomnia, have nightmares, or become anxious and jittery for fear an attack might happen again. Some eat tons of junk food to calm their nerves while others lose their appetite altogether.

Sometimes the body's response to violence can be more chronic and long term. Victims can feel insecure, depressed, or numb. They may isolate themselves

At least 94 percent of women who are raped experience symptoms of PTSD during the two weeks following the attack. A third of these women contemplate suicide.

from loved ones or stay housebound for long periods of time. Many victims become suicidal or suffer from post-traumatic stress disorder (PTSD). People who have PTSD may feel afraid, tense, or paranoid even when they are not in danger.

Recovering from a traumatic event—especially a violent one—can take months or even years. But hope is not lost and rehabilitation is not impossible. There are a number of ways to work through what happened. Many options can be engaged in simultaneously for optimal results.

SOOTHE THE MIND AND BODY

One of the simplest and quickest ways to "medicate" a problem without actually taking prescription drugs is by activating the mind via healthy distractions. Sure, this might seem like cheating or feel like a chore at first. But replaying a violent event can damage healthy thinking processes, not to mention lower confidence and self-esteem.

As with every step in the healing process, it's important to start slow. Listen to peaceful or upbeat music, meditate on your own or with the help of a guided meditation app, watch your favorite movies, or take up a hobby like woodworking, drawing, or pottery. Completing a creative project—and channeling emotions through art—can do wonders for the spirit.

If those activities feel a little too much like avoidance, try journaling in a diary about your feelings or writing poetry or short stories based on your situation. Read novels featuring a character that experiences violence or pick up a memoir that helps you think about your circumstances in a different way. Laurie Halse Anderson's classic *Speak*, Chris Lynch's *Inexcusable*, Julie Ann Peters's *Rage: A Love Story*, and Mindy McGinnis's *The Female of the Species* are a few fiction suggestions. Ask a local librarian for more recommendations.

Beyond occupying the mind, it's also wise to get the body moving. Studies show that most forms of exercise help relieve stress, energize the body, and

Taking a martial arts class is an empowering way to gain confidence, physical strength, and spiritual well-being. Aikido, capoeira, judo, and hapkido are a few examples.

lower metabolism. Running, aerobics, Zumba, Pilates, yoga, and spin classes can be done at the gym or solo. Martial arts classes like taekwondo, jujitsu, or kick-boxing or even hiking in the woods are other options. Self-defense classes teach victims how to mentally and physically defend themselves against bullying, mug-ging, domestic, sexual, and other forms of physical as-sault. Most are inexpensive and are taught by certified instructors. Some are for women only. Others are open to men and women or are geared toward a specific group, such as members of the LGBTQ community.

HOW TO FORM HEALTHY RELATIONSHIPS

Learning to be alone—especially after experiencing or witnessing a trauma—can seem like an uphill battle. But knowing how to stand on your own is essential to living a strong and productive life. Jumping into new friendships or relationships before you're ready can be detrimental because you might fall back into old habits. On the other hand, trusting yourself to form new bonds is key to your recovery. The following are a few tips on how to form healthy relationships:

- When you feel ready, take it slow. Don't jump right in. Moving too fast can incite panic.
- If your old friends have proven to be solid pals, don't ditch them for someone new. If you do, they might not be there if or when you need them next.
- When forming new bonds, trust is a must in order for both people to feel safe and for the relationship to last. Keep the lines of communication open. Express feelings, but don't be afraid to hold back if you're feeling uncomfortable.
- If you're helping a friend through trauma, be a good listener. After all, relationships are about two people, not just one person yammering on.
- Learn to keep promises and secrets, unless given permission to share with others. Expect the same from your partner.
- Know that arguments in any relationship are natural. But yelling, manipulation, and any kind of violence are inexcusable—even if it happens once.

Whichever method of healing feels right to you, be sure to also maintain a healthy diet and get enough sleep. While it may seem like it's unrelated, what you put in your stomach has everything to do with how you feel inside and out. Drinking sugary sodas and eating high-fat, calorie-dense foods can sap energy levels and cause sluggishness. Drugs and alcohol are also off limits. While illicit substances might numb the senses and help you forget what happened in the short term, they also exacerbate your worries, lower your defenses, and leave you vulnerable to future attacks.

GO THE PROFESSIONAL ROUTE

Coping with mental or physical trauma can have long-term psychological effects. So while you're doing healthy things like exercising and eating nutrient-rich foods, you also need to ensure the abuse won't permanently impact the way you think. Your peers are a great go-to resource for comfort and support, but they often lack sufficient experience and perspective. Sometimes talking to a parent or guardian isn't enough either. That certainly won't work if he or she is the abuser.

In many cases, seeking the help of a counselor is a worthwhile direction to follow. A therapist can listen and be empathetic but also be objective. They can provide thoughtful advice and can act as an advocate if the situation gets increasingly out of control. Most importantly, therapists and psychiatrists are professionals. This means they are trained to deal with seemingly

Talk therapy isn't right for everyone. But sometimes just knowing there is someone out there who will listen unconditionally is worth its weight in gold.

insurmountable problems you might not be able to handle on your own.

There are many types of counselors, depending on the severity of the issue. The following are a few of the options you might consider when researching where to go for help:

- A guidance counselor works in a school and can give advice about social issues such as bullying, peer pressure, dating, and sex. Most guidance counselors do not have medical degrees.

- A therapist is a professional who helps individuals work though and solve personal problems. Many have private practices or offer group-therapy sessions.
- A psychologist is a therapist who has a graduate degree in psychology, usually a doctoral degree. Psychologists use advanced forms of treatment such as cognitive behavioral therapy, psychotherapy, and substance abuse counseling.
- A licensed clinical social worker helps clients cope with problems such as abuse, addiction, and mental illness by providing counseling and connecting clients with health service providers. They not only address psychological issues, but they also work with people to examine their relationships, family history, and work environment in order to identify ways to solve a particular challenge.
- A psychiatrist diagnoses, treats, and attempts to prevent mental, emotional, and behavioral disorders. Most psychiatrists use talk therapy to work through issues with their patients. Psychiatrists can also prescribe prescription drugs, such as antidepressants or mood stabilizers.

No matter which type of professional you choose, be sure to assess whether the person is the right fit for your personality. If you don't feel comfortable talking openly and honestly about your feelings and fears, find another counselor or therapist.

10 GREAT QUESTIONS TO ASK A THERAPIST

1. What if I feel guilt or shame about what happened?
2. What if I still have feelings for or love my abuser?
3. If I have been abused, do I need to take legal action and, if so, how do I do that?
4. If I've been sexually abused, do I need to get an STD or pregnancy test?
5. Will I ever get over the pain?
6. What if I have suicidal thoughts?
7. How can I help a friend who I know is being abused?
8. What do I do next if I've tried all the preventative steps and I'm still being abused?
9. What if I tell people about the abuse and no one believes me?
10. If I know someone who is an abuser, how can I make sure that person gets help?

CHAPTER FIVE

TAKING ACTION

At the beginning of her sophomore year in college at New York City's Columbia University, Emma Sulkowicz was busy planning orientation activities for the school's incoming freshman class. She had decided upon a major, joined a coed fraternity, and was excited for classes to get underway. But one night, after a party for orientation leaders, Sulkowicz was assaulted by Paul Nungesser, a fellow student. While the sex started out as consensual, Sulkowicz says it quickly turned violent. She claims it was rape.

Initially, Sulkowicz didn't report the incident. But after two other women told her Nungesser had harassed them, she decided to press charges. In 2013, she filed a claim with the university. After six months of deliberation, a panel found in favor of Nungesser, who insisted the charges were fabricated. Though Sulkowicz appealed, a dean refused to overturn the verdict.

Sulkowicz spent more than a year distraught by what had happened. But in her final year at Columbia, she decided to do something about it. As part of her senior arts thesis, she lugged around a fifty-pound

Emma Sulkowicz's mattress project inspired the Carrying the Weight Together movement. After graduating, she has continued to protest violence against women and bring much-needed attention to the cause.

(twenty-three-kilogram) mattress whenever she was on campus to symbolize her psychological and emotional burden. She even dragged it on stage when she got her diploma during the May 2015 graduation ceremony. The yearlong performance piece not only attracted hundreds of local supporters who helped carry the mattress throughout the year, it also sparked an international movement called Carrying the Weight Together. Protests to raise awareness about rape and violence against women were held on more than 130 college campuses.

Emma Sulkowicz's college experience was marred by sexual violence. But instead of letting it beat her, she turned the horrific event into an opportunity to incite change. If you or someone you know is a survivor of verbal, emotional, or physical violence, there are ways to take action, educate others, and help prevent similar situations from impacting more women and girls.

STAY INFORMED

The most surefire method to confronting violence against women is to know the facts. Keep up to speed with what's going on in your community and around the world by reading or listening to the news and staying informed of women's issues

Protesting violence against women is essential so that perpetrators can be held accountable. This protest took place in London in 2015.

and local, national, and international events. If there's something you don't understand, ask a teacher, librarian, or knowledgeable adult to explain it to you.

Then, figure out what you don't know and do more research. If you're interested in finding out more about a particular issue related to violence against women, there are plenty of organizations and online resources that can help. Here are a few reputable and nonbi-ased places to start.

- **National Sexual Violence Resource Center** hosts online courses, videos, podcasts, and information about rape on college campuses, resources for immigrants facing sexual violence, statistics on alcohol-facilitated sexual assault, and other issues.
- **VAWnet.org** is an online database that contains thousands of vetted articles, videos, photographs, and materials on gender-based violence and related issues. Research categories include Engagement & Collaboration, Intervention & Prevention, Management & Sustainability, Policy & Systems Advocacy, and Research & Statistics.
- **Rape, Assault and Incest National Network (RAINN)** is the largest anti-sexual violence organization in the United States. The group has a website (www.rainn.org) where you can research federal laws or laws in your state that protect women. It is also home to a self-guided educational program that aims to help individuals recover and heal after a sexual assault.
- **Love Is Respect** is an organization and website that posts information about teen dating violence. The site also has a live chat option that is available twenty-four hours a day, seven days a week, and a free national hotline staffed by trained professionals.

LAWS THAT PROTECT WOMEN AND GIRLS

Many U.S. states have laws that aim to protect women and girls against violence. There are federal laws, too. For more detailed information, you can check out the websites ChangingOurCampus.org or WomensHealth.gov, two resource centers supported by the Office on Violence Against Women and the Office on Women's Health. Relevant federal laws include:

- **Title IX is a section of the United States Education Amendments of 1972. It states, in part, that "no one in the United States shall, on the basis of their gender, be excluded from participation in, be denied the benefits of, or be subjected to discrimination under any education program or activity receiving Federal financial assistance."**
- **The Family Violence Prevention and Services Act (FVPSA) provides the main federal funding to help victims of domestic violence and their children. Signed into law in 1984, it secures grants for crisis centers, shelters, and local programs that teach people ways to prevent violence against women.**
- **The Violence Against Women Act (VAWA) was the first major law to help local and national government agencies and victim advocates work together to fight domestic violence, sexual assault, and other types of violence against women. Enacted in 1994, it created punishment guidelines for certain crimes and set money aside for violence prevention and treatment programs.**

- **Childhelp** is a nonprofit that helps the victims of child abuse through education, treatment, and prevention programs. Their website has resources and articles about physical abuse, sexual assault, and how to report it. It also operates a 24/7 hotline that provides crisis counseling for survivors (1-800-422-4453).

RAISE AWARENESS

Once you have become more informed about violence against women and girls, the next step in stopping the epidemic from spreading is to educate and raise awareness in others. Thanks to the internet, doing so is easy. Share informative articles, links to trustworthy websites, and petitions advocating change on Facebook, Snapchat, and Twitter. Interview students or local people in your community who are working to combat the issue. Make a documentary and post it on YouTube.

If you or someone you know has experienced violence, the internet is a quick and useful tool to get help and incite change.

CHECH YOUR ATTITUDE

There are many ways to get involved to prevent violence against women and girls. Begin by taking a deep look at your own attitudes. After all, before you can influence others in a positive way, you have to first ensure your behavior is on track. Ask yourself these questions to determine where and how you might improve.

- Will I do what it takes to make sure violence doesn't happen to me or to those I love?
- Do I stand by and say nothing when someone makes a derogatory comment about a person of color, an immigrant, or a member of the LGBTQ community?
- Am I willing to listen and be open to change if a friend points out that my behavior is sexist or misogynistic?
- Do I recognize my own privilege or biases when thinking about issues concerning women and girls?
- If I have been responsible for violence against women and girls, am I willing to get help?

If you are a survivor of bullying, physical assault, or rape, consider sharing your story, either in person during a storytelling competition or poetry slam, via a personal blog, or in an online support group. For example, After Silence (www.aftersilence.org) is just one of many nonprofit organizations that host message boards and chat rooms for rape, sexual assault, and sexual abuse survivors. Remember to vet whichever website you choose and use caution about what information you post.

As the old adage goes, if you see something, say something. If you witness inappropriate behavior directed at a woman or girl or hear someone making sexist jokes or bragging about an assault, speak up. Don't let the perpetrator get away with it. Staying silent normalizes violence and makes it seem OK. Voicing your disapproval and showing others the right way to behave not only prevents violence from taking place, it can also chip away at others' tolerance for predatory behavior.

VOLUNTEER AND ADVOCATE FOR CHANGE

Unfortunately, violence against women and girls isn't going away anytime soon. But there are countless ways to advocate for change. Volunteering at a domestic violence shelter, a sexual assault hotline, or at a rape crisis center means that you're not only providing direct assistance to battered women in your area, but you're also getting involved in a community of others who share similar goals.

If you're interested in more far-reaching change, contact your congressman, congresswoman, or representative to find out how you can lobby for laws to help survivors of violence. Sign and circulate online petitions that protect women. Or get a part-time job or internship with a social worker or legal aid group to learn more about what you can do for the cause.

Whatever you choose to do, whether it's in person or online, find a way to speak out. In 2017, the #MeToo

In Tyngsborough, Massachusetts, Empire Beauty School student stylists are taught how to identify signs of domestic violence and learn the resources available to help those in need.

movement on social media let millions of women share their stories about abuse. It helped vulnerable women feel more empowered and led to a spate of sexual abusers being held responsible for their actions.

Finally, embolden your community and make sure it's the best it can be. Never tolerate sexist or aggressive behavior toward women and girls in yourself, your friend group, at school, or at home. Everyone can make a difference in how violence against women and girls is viewed in society and how offenders are punished.

coercion The process of achieving a result using threats or force.

date rape drug A class of medication placed secretly in the food or drink of a potential victim to make that person confused and vulnerable to sexual assault or rape.

derogatory Expressing a low opinion of someone or showing a lack of respect for them.

discrimination The practice of treating a person or group of people differently from other people and often unfairly.

domestic violence Violent or aggressive behavior within the home, typically involving the violent abuse of a spouse or intimate partner.

dowry In certain cultures, when a wife's family gives money or property to the husband's family after the couple gets married.

egregious Very bad.

exploitation The act of taking advantage of another person.

heterosexual Someone who is sexually attracted to people of the opposite sex.

lesbian A woman who is sexually attracted to women.

manipulation The act of controlling someone in a selfish or unfair way, usually through inappropriate behavior or language.

molest To touch someone in a sexual and improper way.

perpetrator A person who is responsible for doing something that is illegal or wrong.

post-traumatic stress disorder (PTSD) A mental condition that affects a person who has had a traumatic or violent experience that is usually characterized by depression, anxiety, and paranoia.

prevalent Common or widespread.

rape When someone forces another person to have sex against that person's will and without consent.

retaliation The act of getting revenge against someone.

sadistic Very cruel or causing pain.

sexism Unfair treatment of people because of their sex or gender.

slut-shame To stigmatize or harass a woman for engaging in behavior judged to be sexually provocative.

stalking Following, watching, or bothering constantly in a way that is frightening or dangerous.

transgender Of or relating to a person whose gender does not correspond to the sex they were assigned at birth.

Break the Cycle
PO Box 66165
Washington, DC 20035
(202) 849-6289
Website: https://www.breakthecycle.org
Facebook: @breakthecycle
Twitter: @BreaktheCycleDV
Break the Cycle is a national nonprofit organiza-
tion that provides programs to end dating abuse
aimed at young people ages twelve to twenty-four.

Canadian Women's Foundation
133 Richmond Street W, Suite 504
Toronto, ON M5H 2L3
Canada
(416) 365-1444
Website: http://www.canadianwomen.org
Twitter: @cdnwomenfdn
This organization is Canada's only national foundation dedicated to empowering women and girls to
move out of violence and poverty and into confidence and leadership.

Department of Justice Office on Violence Against
Women
145 N Street NE, Suite 10W.121
Washington, DC 20530
(202) 307-6026

Website: https://www.justice.gov/ovw
This branch of the U.S. government works to reduce
violence against women by administering justice
on the federal level and strengthening services
to victims of domestic violence, dating violence,
sexual assault, and stalking.

LoveIsRespect.org
(866) 331-9474
Website: http://www.loveisrespect.org
Facebook: @loveisrespectpage
Text: loveis to 22522
Tumblr/Twitter: @loveisrespect
Launched in 2007, this national hotline was the first
twenty-four-hour resource for teens experiencing
dating violence or abuse.

National Domestic Violence Hotline
PO Box 161810
Austin, TX 78716
(800) 799-SAFE
Website: http://www.thehotline.org
This hotline provides immediate support to victims
of abuse. It operates twenty-four hours a day and
is staffed by trained volunteers who can provide
crisis-intervention information and referral services
in more than 200 languages.

National Online Resource Center for Violence Against
Women (VAWnet)
6400 Flank Drive, Suite 1300

Harrisburg, PA 17112
(800) 537-2238
Website: http://vawnet.org
Facebook/Twitter: @VAWnet
VAWnet was created in 1995 by the National Re-
    source Center on Domestic Violence. It is a com-
    prehensive collection of online resources and a
    searchable database containing information about
    gender-based violence and intersecting issues,
    such as homelessness, racial justice, criminal jus-
    tice, and child welfare.

National Organization for Women (NOW)
1100 H Street NW, Suite 300
Washington, DC 20005
(202) 628-8669
Website: http://now.org
Facebook/Twitter: @NationalNOW
The National Organization for Women is the largest
    women's advocacy organization in the United
    States, with more than 500,000 members and 500
    local chapters. The group educates the public
    and takes action on a variety of issues, including
    rape and domestic violence, reproductive rights
    and abortion, lesbian rights, gender equality in the
    workplace, and racial or sexual discrimination.

Bickerstaff, Linda. *Violence Against Women: Public Health and Human Rights* (A Young Woman's Guide to Contemporary Issues). New York, NY: Rosen Publishing, 2010.

Burton, Bonnie. *Girls Against Girls: Why We Are Mean to Each Other and How We Can Change.* San Francisco, CA: Zest Books, 2009.

Byers, Ann. *Sexual Assault and Abuse* (Confronting Violence Against Women). New York, NY: Rosen Publishing, 2016.

Heing, Bridey. *Critical Perspectives on Sexual Harassment and Gender Violence* (Analyzing the Issues). New York, NY: Enslow Publishing, 2018.

Henneberg, Susan. *I Have Been Raped. Now What?* (Teen Life 411). New York, NY: Rosen Publishing, 2016.

Hiber, Amanda, ed. *Sexual Violence* (Opposing Viewpoints). Farmington Hills, MI: Greenhaven Press, 2014.

Idzikowski, Lisa. *Honor Killings* (Global Viewpoints). New York, NY: Greenhaven Publishing, 2018.

La Bella, Laura. *Dating Violence* (Confronting Violence Against Women). New York, NY: Rosen Publishing, 2016.

Lohmann, Raychelle Cassada, and Sheela Raja. *The Sexual Trauma Workbook for Teen Girls*. Oakland, CA: New Harbinger Publications, Inc., 2016.

Lowery, Zoe. *Gender-Based Violence and Women's*

Rights (Women in the World). New York, NY: Rosen YA, 2018.

Marriott, Emma. *Violence Against Women* (Behind the News). New York, NY: Crabtree Publishing, 2016.

Merino, Noel, ed. *Violence Against Women* (Current Controversies). Farmington Hills, MI: Greenhaven Press, 2016.

Meyer, Terry Teague. *Sexual Trafficking and Modern-Day Slavery* (Confronting Violence Against Women). New York, NY: Rosen Publishing, 2016

Miller, Jody. *Getting Played: African American Girls, Urban Inequality, and Gendered Violence.* New York, NY: New York University Press, 2008.

O'Neill, Louise. *Asking for It.* New York, NY: Quercus, 2016.

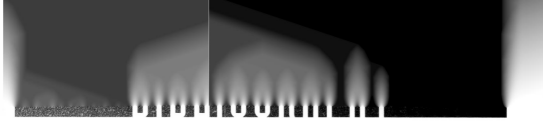

Battered Women's Support Services. "The Facts on Violence Against Women." Retrieved September 6, 2017. http://www.bwss.org/resources/information -on-abuse/numbers-are-people-too/#_ftn15.

Braunschweiger, Amy. "Witness: Raped in the U.S. Military, Retaliated Against for Life." HRW.org, May 19, 2016. https://www.hrw.org/news/2016/05/19/witness -raped-us-military-retaliated-against-life.

Brown, Anna, and Eileen Patten. "The Narrowing, but Persistent, Gender Gap in Pay." Pew Research Center, April 3, 2017. http://www.pewresearch.org /fact-tank/2017/04/03/gender-pay-gap-facts.

Browne, Ryan. "First Marine Tied to 'Marines United' Facebook Group Court-Martialed." CNN, July 10, 2017. http://www.cnn.com/2017/07/10/politics /marines-united-facebook-group-court-martial/index .html

Centers for Disease Control and Prevention. "Intimate Partner Violence: Risk and Protective Factors." August 22, 2017. https://www.cdc.gov /violenceprevention/intimatepartnerviolence /riskprotectivefactors.html.

Ghafoerkhan, Olivia. *Sexual Assault: The Ultimate Teen Guide*. Lanham, MD: Rowman & Littlefield, 2017.

LoveIsRespect.org. "Is This Abuse?" Retrieved September 6, 2017. http://www.loveisrespect.org/is-this -abuse.

National Coalition Against Domestic Violence. "Dynamics of Abuse." Retrieved September 6, 2017. http://

ncadv.org/learn-more/what-is-domestic-violence
/dynamics-of-abuse.
Nerhaugen, Ruth. "'I Thought I Was Going to Lose My
Life,' MN Woman Recalls Violent Teen Relationship."
River Falls Journal, August 23, 2017. http://www
.riverfallsjournal.com/news/4316542-i-thought-i-was
-going-lose-my-life-mn-woman-recalls-violent-teen
-relationship.
Office on Violence Against Women. "Domestic Violence." U.S. Department of Justice, June 16, 2017.
https://www.justice.gov/ovw/domestic-violence.
RAINN. "Safety and Prevention." Retrieved September
6, 2017. https://www.rainn.org/safety-prevention.
Robinson, Lisa. "Rihanna in Cuba: The Cover Story."
Vanity Fair, November 2015. https://www.vanityfair
.com/hollywood/2015/10/rihanna-cover-cuba
-annie-leibovitz.
Safe Horizon. "Domestic Violence Statistics and Facts."
Retrieved September 6, 2017. https://www
.safehorizon.org/get-informed/domestic-violence
-statistics-facts/#our-impact.
Taylor, Kate. "Columbia Settles with Student Cast as
a Rapist in Mattress Art Project." *New York Times*,
July 14, 2017. https://www.nytimes.com
/2017/07/14/nyregion/columbia-settles-with
-student-cast-as-a-rapist-in-mattress-art-project
.html?mcubz=3&_r=1.
United Nations Department of Public Education. "Unite
to End Violence Against Women: Fact Sheet." February 2008. http://www.un.org/en/women/endviolence
/pdf/VAW.pdf.

United Nations Entity for Gender Equality and the Empowerment of Women. "Virtual Knowledge Centre to End Violence Against Women and Girls." Retrieved September 6, 2017. http://www.endvawnow.org/en/articles/300-causes-protective-and-risk-factors-.html.

UN Women. "Facts and Figures: Ending Violence Against Women." February 2016. http://www.unwomen.org/en/what-we-do/ending-violence-against-women/facts-and-figures#notes.

VAWnet.org. "Domestic Violence: Understanding the Basics." Retrieved September 6, 2017. http://vawnet.org/elearning/DVBasics/player.html.

Walters, Joanna. "Derogatory Discharge Papers Blight Lives of Military Who Report Sexual Assault." *The Guardian*, May 19, 2016. https://www.theguardian.com/us-news/2016/may/19/derogatory-discharge-papers-military-sexual-assault.

WomensHealth.gov. "Violence Against Women." Office on Women's Health, September 30, 2015. https://www.womenshealth.gov/violence-against-women/types-of-violence/domestic-intimate-partner-violence.html.

World Health Organization. "Violence Against Women: Fact Sheet." November 2016. http://www.who.int/mediacentre/factsheets/fs239/en.

ABOUT THE AUTHOR

Alexis Burling spent many years as an editor and contributor to Scholastic's preeminent classroom magazines, including *Storyworks, Choices*, and *SuperScience*. She has written many books and articles for kids and teens on a variety of topics ranging from current events and career advice to biographies of famous people. Her latest books include *Race in the Criminal Justice System* and a biography of scientist Robert Boyle. Burling lives among the trees with her husband in Portland, Oregon.

PHOTO CREDITS

Cover, pp. 10, 12 Mixmike/E+/Getty Images; pp. 5, 20 Pacific Press/LightRocket/Getty Images; pp. 7, 16, 26, 34, 43 Agnieszka Marcinska/Shutterstock.com; p. 8 Gilbert Carrasquillo/FilmMagic /Getty Images; p. 14 PeopleImages/E+/Getty Images; p. 19 Catherine Ledner/Taxi/Getty Images; p. 22 NurPhoto/Getty Images; p. 23 Mark Scoggins/Photolibrary/Getty Images; p. 27 gawrav/E+/Getty Images; p. 29 Tim Robberts/Taxi/Getty Images; p. 32 asiseeit/E+/Getty Images; pp. 35, 40 Tetra Images/Getty Images; p. 37 track5/E+/Getty Images; p. 44 Andrew Burton /Getty Images; p. 45 Keith Mayhew/Alamy Stock Photo; p. 48 Brendan O'Sullivan/Photolibrary/Getty Images; p. 51 Boston Globe/Getty Images.

Design: Michael Moy; Layout: Ellina Litmanovich;
Editor: Amelie von Zumbusch; Photo Research: Nicole Baker